CROCK·POT®

· THE ORIGINAL SLOW COOKER ·

Family

FAVORITES

pil

Publications International, Ltd.

Pictured on the front cover: Slow Cooker Pizza Casserole *(page 76).*
Pictured on the back cover *(left to right):* Chorizo Chili *(page 26)* and Easy Parmesan
Chicken *(page 46).*

ISBN: 978-1-64030-129-0

Library of Congress Control Number: 2014936679

Manufactured in China.

8 7 6 5 4 3 2 1

Publications International, Ltd.

Contents

Slow Cooking 101   4

Soups and Chilies   8

Pasta Dinners   32

Kids' Favorites   56

Satisfying Sides   80

Delicious Desserts   106

Index   124

page 22

page 46

page 58

Slow Cooking 101

Slow Cooker Sizes

Smaller **CROCK-POT®** slow cookers—such as 1- to 3½-quart models—are the perfect size for cooking for singles, a couple, or empty-nesters (and also for serving dips).

While medium-size **CROCK-POT®** slow cookers (those holding somewhere between 3 quarts and 5 quarts) will easily cook enough food at a time to feed a small family, they're also convenient for holiday side dishes or appetizers.

Large **CROCK-POT®** slow cookers are great for large family dinners, holiday entertaining, and potluck suppers. A 6- to 7-quart model is ideal if you like to make meals in advance, or have dinner tonight and store leftovers for another day.

Types of Slow Cookers

Current **CROCK-POT®** slow cookers come equipped with many different features and benefits, from auto cook programs to stovetop-safe stoneware to timed programming. Visit **www.crockpot.com** to find the **CROCK-POT®** slow cooker that best suits your needs.

How you plan to use a **CROCK-POT®** slow cooker may affect the model you choose to purchase. For everyday cooking, choose a size large enough to serve your family. If you plan to use the **CROCK-POT®** slow cooker primarily for entertaining, choose one of the larger sizes. Basic **CROCK-POT®** slow cookers can hold as little as 16 ounces or as much as 7 quarts. The smallest sizes are great for keeping dips warm on a buffet, while the larger sizes can more readily fit large quantities of food and larger roasts.

Cooking, Stirring, and Food Safety

CROCK-POT® slow cookers are safe to leave unattended. The outer heating base may get hot as it cooks, but it should not pose a fire hazard. The heating element in the heating base functions at a low wattage and is safe for your countertops.

Your **CROCK-POT®** slow cooker should be filled about one-half to three-fourths full for most recipes unless otherwise

instructed. Lean meats such as chicken or pork tenderloin will cook faster than meats with more connective tissue and fat such as beef chuck or pork shoulder. Bone-in meats will take longer than boneless cuts. Typical **CROCK-POT®** slow cooker dishes take approximately 7 to 8 hours to reach the simmer point on LOW and about 3 to 4 hours on HIGH. Once the vegetables and meat start to simmer and braise, their flavors will fully blend and meat will become fall-off-the-bone tender.

According to the USDA, all bacteria are killed at a temperature of 165°F. It's important to follow the recommended cooking times and not to open the lid often, especially early in the cooking process when heat is building up inside the unit. If you need to open the lid to check on your food or are adding additional ingredients, remember to allow additional cooking time if necessary to ensure food is cooked through and tender.

Large **CROCK-POT®** slow cookers, the 6- to 7-quart sizes, may benefit with a quick stir halfway through cook time to help distribute heat and promote even cooking. It's usually unnecessary to stir at all, as even ½ cup liquid will help to distribute heat and the stoneware is the perfect medium for holding food at an even temperature throughout the cooking process.

Oven-Safe

All **CROCK-POT®** slow cooker removable stoneware inserts may (without their lids) be used safely in ovens at up to 400°F.

Also, all **CROCK-POT®** slow cookers are microwavable without their lids. If you own another brand slow cooker, please refer to your owner's manual for specific stoneware cooking medium tolerances.

Frozen Food

Frozen food or partially frozen food can be successfully cooked in a **CROCK-POT®** slow cooker; however, it will require longer cooking time than the same recipe made with fresh food. It's almost always preferable to thaw frozen food prior to placing it in the **CROCK-POT®** slow cooker. Using an instant-read thermometer is recommended to ensure meat is fully cooked through.

Pasta and Rice

If you're converting a recipe that calls for uncooked pasta, cook the pasta on the stovetop just until slightly tender before adding to the **CROCK-POT®** slow cooker. If you are converting a recipe that calls for cooked rice, stir in raw rice with other ingredients; add ¼ cup extra liquid per ¼ cup of raw rice.

Beans

Beans must be softened completely before combining with sugar and/or acidic foods. Sugar and acid have a hardening effect on beans and will prevent softening. Fully cooked canned beans may be used as a substitute for dried beans.

(page 42)

Vegetables

Root vegetables often cook more slowly than meat. Cut vegetables accordingly to cook at the same rate as meat—large or small, or lean versus marbled—and place near the sides or bottom of the stoneware to facilitate cooking.

Herbs

Fresh herbs add flavor and color when added at the end of the cooking cycle; if added at the beginning, many fresh herbs' flavor will dissipate over long cook times. Ground and/or dried herbs and spices work well in slow cooking

and may be added at the beginning, and for dishes with shorter cook times, hearty fresh herbs such as rosemary and thyme hold up well. The flavor power of all herbs and spices can vary greatly depending on their particular strength and shelf life. Use chili powders and garlic powder sparingly, as these can sometimes intensify over the long cook times. Always taste the finished dish and correct seasonings including salt and pepper.

Liquids

It is not necessary to use more than ½ to 1 cup liquid in most instances since juices in meats and vegetables are retained more in slow cooking than in conventional cooking. Excess liquid can be cooked down and concentrated after slow cooking on the stovetop or by removing meat and vegetables from stoneware, stirring in one of the following thickeners, and setting the slow cooker to HIGH. Cook on HIGH for approximately 15 minutes or until juices are thickened.

Flour: All-purpose flour is often used to thicken soups or stews. Stir cold water into the flour in a small bowl until smooth. With the **CROCK-POT®** slow cooker on HIGH, whisk the flour mixture into the liquid in the **CROCK-POT®** slow cooker. Cover; cook on HIGH 15 minutes or until the mixture is thickened.

Cornstarch: Cornstarch gives sauces a clear, shiny appearance; it's used most often for sweet dessert sauces and stir-fry sauces. Stir cold water into the cornstarch in a small bowl until the cornstarch dissolves. Quickly stir this mixture into the liquid in the **CROCK-POT®** slow cooker; the sauce will thicken as soon as the liquid boils. Cornstarch breaks down with too much heat, so never add it at the beginning of the slow cooking process, and turn off the heat as soon as the sauce thickens.

Arrowroot: Arrowroot (or arrowroot flour) comes from the root of a tropical plant that is dried and ground to a powder; it produces a thick, clear sauce. Those who are allergic to wheat often use it in place of flour. Place arrowroot in a small bowl or cup and stir in cold water until the mixture is smooth. Quickly stir this mixture into the liquid in the **CROCK-POT®** slow cooker. Arrowroot thickens below the boiling point, so it even works well in a **CROCK-POT®** slow cooker on LOW. Too much stirring can break down an arrowroot mixture.

Tapioca: Tapioca is a starchy substance extracted from the root of the cassava plant. Its greatest advantage is that it withstands long cooking, making it an ideal choice for slow cooking. Add it at the beginning of cooking and you'll get a clear, thickened sauce in the finished dish. Dishes using tapioca as a thickener are best cooked on the LOW setting; tapioca may become stringy when boiled for a long time.

Milk

Milk, cream, and sour cream break down during extended cooking. When possible, add them during the last 15 to 30 minutes of cooking, until just heated through. Condensed soups may be substituted for milk and can cook for extended times.

(page 24)

Fish

Fish is delicate and should be stirred in gently during the last 15 to 30 minutes of cooking time. Cover and cook just until cooked through and serve immediately.

Baked Goods

If you wish to prepare bread, cakes, or pudding cakes in a **CROCK-POT®** slow cooker, you may want to purchase a covered, vented metal cake pan accessory for your **CROCK-POT®** slow cooker. You can also use any straight-sided soufflé dish or deep cake pan that will fit into the stoneware of your unit. Baked goods can be prepared directly in the stoneware; however, they can be a little difficult to remove from the insert, so follow the recipe directions carefully.

Easy Chili (page 24)

Potato Soup (page 30)

Soups and Chilies

Simmered Split Pea Soup (page 28)

Hearty Sausage and Tortellini Soup

3 hot Italian sausages,
    casings removed

3 sweet Italian sausages,
    casings removed

5 cups chicken broth

1 can (about 14 ounces)
    diced tomatoes with
    garlic and oregano

1 can (about 8 ounces)
    tomato sauce

1 large onion, chopped

2 medium carrots, chopped

1 teaspoon seasoned salt

½ teaspoon Italian
    seasoning

¼ teaspoon black pepper

1 package (9 ounces)
    refrigerated cheese
    tortellini

1 medium zucchini,
    chopped

2 cups broccoli, chopped

1. Cook sausages in large skillet over medium-high heat 8 to 10 minutes. Drain fat. Add sausages, broth, diced tomatoes, tomato sauce, onion, carrots, seasoned salt, Italian seasoning and pepper to **CROCK-POT**® slow cooker. Cover; cook on LOW 6 to 8 hours or on HIGH 3 to 4 hours.

2. Meanwhile, cook tortellini according to package directions. Add tortellini, zucchini and broccoli to **CROCK-POT**® slow cooker during last 15 to 20 minutes of cooking.

Makes 6 to 8 servings

Classic Chili

1½ pounds ground beef
1½ cups chopped onion
1 cup chopped green bell
   pepper
2 cloves garlic, minced
3 cans (about 15 ounces
   each) dark red kidney
   beans, rinsed and
   drained
2 cans (about 15 ounces
   each) tomato sauce
1 can (about 14 ounces)
   diced tomatoes
2 to 3 teaspoons chili
   powder
1 to 2 teaspoons ground
   mustard
¾ teaspoon dried basil
½ teaspoon black pepper
1 to 2 dried red chiles
   (optional)

1. Brown beef, onion, bell pepper and garlic in large skillet over medium-high heat, stirring to break up meat. Remove beef mixture to **CROCK-POT®** slow cooker using slotted spoon.

2. Add beans, tomato sauce, tomatoes, chili powder, mustard, basil, black pepper and chiles, if desired, to **CROCK-POT®** slow cooker; mix well. Cover; cook on LOW 8 to 10 hours or on HIGH 4 to 5 hours. If used, remove chiles before serving.

Makes 6 servings

Asian Sugar Snap Pea Soup

2 tablespoons peanut or canola oil

4 to 5 new potatoes, coarsely chopped

2 green onions, chopped

1 medium carrot, thinly sliced

1 stalk celery, thinly sliced

1 leek, thinly sliced

5 cups water

2 cups broccoli, washed and cut into florets

1 tablespoon lemon juice

1 tablespoon soy sauce

1 teaspoon ground coriander

1 teaspoon ground cumin

1 teaspoon prepared horseradish

⅛ teaspoon ground red pepper

1 cup fresh sugar snap peas, shelled, rinsed and drained

4 cups cooked brown rice

1. Heat oil in large skillet over medium heat. Add potatoes, green onions, carrot, celery and leek; cook and stir 10 to 12 minutes or until vegetables begin to soften.

2. Remove to **CROCK-POT®** slow cooker. Add water, broccoli, lemon juice, soy sauce, coriander, cumin, horseradish and ground red pepper. Cover; cook on LOW 5 to 6 hours or on HIGH 2 to 3 hours.

3. Stir in peas. Cover; cook on HIGH 15 minutes or until peas are crisp-tender. To serve, portion rice into four bowls. Ladle soup over rice and serve immediately.

Makes 4 servings

Weeknight Chili

1 pound ground beef or
   turkey
1 package (about 1 ounce)
   chili seasoning mix
1 can (about 15 ounces) red
   kidney beans, rinsed
   and drained
1 can (about 14 ounces)
   diced tomatoes with
   mild green chiles
1 can (8 ounces) tomato
   sauce
1 cup (4 ounces) shredded
   Cheddar cheese
   (optional)
  Chopped green onion
   (optional)

1. Brown beef in large skillet over medium-high heat 6 to 8 minutes, stirring to break up meat. Drain fat. Stir in seasoning mix.

2. Place beef mixture, beans, tomatoes and tomato sauce in **CROCK-POT**® slow cooker. Cover; cook on LOW 4 to 6 hours or on HIGH 2 to 3 hours. Garnish with cheese and green onion.

Makes 4 servings

Mother's Sausage and Vegetable Soup

1 can (about 15 ounces)
   black beans, rinsed
   and drained
1 can (about 14 ounces)
   diced tomatoes
1 can (10¾ ounces)
   condensed cream
   of mushroom soup,
   undiluted
½ pound smoked turkey
   sausage, cut into
   ½-inch slices
2 cups diced potato
1 cup chopped onion
1 cup chopped red bell
   pepper
½ cup water
2 teaspoons prepared
   horseradish
2 teaspoons honey
1 teaspoon dried basil

Combine beans, tomatoes, soup, turkey sausage, potato, onion, pepper, water, horseradish, honey and basil in **CROCK-POT®** slow cooker; stir to blend. Cover; cook on LOW 7 to 8 hours.

Makes 6 to 8 servings

Chili with Turkey and Beans

2 cans (about 15 ounces
  each) red kidney
  beans, rinsed and
  drained

2 cans (about 14 ounces
  each) whole tomatoes,
  drained

1 pound cooked ground
  turkey

1 can (about 15 ounces)
  black beans, rinsed
  and drained

1 can (12 ounces) tomato
  sauce

1 cup finely chopped onion

1 cup finely chopped celery

1 cup finely chopped carrot

½ cup amaretto (optional)

3 tablespoons chili powder

1 tablespoon
  Worcestershire sauce

4 teaspoons ground cumin

2 teaspoons ground red
  pepper

1 teaspoon salt

  Shredded Cheddar
  cheese

Combine kidney beans, whole tomatoes, turkey, black beans, tomato sauce, onion, celery, carrot, amaretto, if desired, chili powder, Worcestershire sauce, cumin, ground red pepper and salt in **CROCK-POT®** slow cooker. Cover; cook on HIGH 7 hours. Top each serving with cheese.

Makes 4 servings

Chicken Tortilla Soup

4 boneless, skinless
    chicken thighs

2 cans (about 14 ounces
    each) diced tomatoes

1 can (4 ounces) chopped
    mild green chiles,
    drained

½ to 1 cup chicken broth

1 yellow onion, diced

2 cloves garlic, minced

1 teaspoon ground cumin

    Salt and black pepper

4 corn tortillas, sliced into
    ¼-inch strips

2 tablespoons chopped
    fresh cilantro

½ cup (2 ounces) shredded
    Monterey Jack cheese

1 avocado, diced and
    tossed with lime juice

    Lime wedges

1. Place chicken in **CROCK-POT®** slow cooker. Combine tomatoes, chiles, ½ cup broth, onion, garlic and cumin in small bowl; stir to blend. Pour mixture over chicken. Cover; cook on LOW 6 hours or on HIGH 3 hours.

2. Remove chicken to cutting board. Shred with two forks. Return to cooking liquid. Add salt, pepper and additional broth, if necessary.

3. Just before serving, add tortillas and cilantro to **CROCK-POT®** slow cooker; stir to blend. Top each serving with cheese, avocado and a squeeze of lime juice.

Makes 4 to 6 servings

Double Thick Potato-Cheese Soup

2 pounds baking potatoes, cut into ½-inch cubes

2 cans (10½ ounces *each*) condensed cream of mushroom soup

1½ cups finely chopped green onions, divided

¼ teaspoon garlic powder

⅛ teaspoon ground red pepper

1½ cups (6 ounces) shredded sharp Cheddar cheese

1 cup (8 ounces) sour cream

1 cup milk

Black pepper

1. Combine potatoes, soup, 1 cup green onions, garlic powder and ground red pepper in **CROCK-POT®** slow cooker. Cover; cook on LOW 8 hours or on HIGH 4 hours.

2. Stir cheese, sour cream and milk into **CROCK-POT®** slow cooker until cheese is melted. Cover; cook on HIGH 10 minutes. Season with black pepper. Garnish with remaining ½ cup green onions.

Makes 6 servings

Easy Chili

(pictured on page 8)

1 teaspoon vegetable oil

1 pound ground beef

1 medium onion, chopped

2 cans (10¾ ounces *each*) condensed tomato soup, undiluted

1 cup water

Salt and black pepper

Chili powder

Shredded Cheddar cheese (optional)

1. Heat oil in large skillet over medium-high heat. Brown beef and onion 6 to 8 minutes, stirring to break up meat. Remove meat mixture to **CROCK-POT®** slow cooker using slotted spoon.

2. Add soup, water, salt, pepper and chili powder to **CROCK-POT®** slow cooker; stir to blend. Cover; cook on LOW 6 to 8 hours. Sprinkle each serving with cheese, if desired.

Makes 4 servings

Double Thick Potato-Cheese Soup

Chorizo Chili

1 pound ground beef

8 ounces bulk raw
   chorizo sausage *or*
   ½ (15-ounce) package
   raw chorizo sausage,
   casings removed*

1 can (about 15 ounces)
   chili beans in chili
   sauce

2 cans (about 14 ounces
   each) chili-style diced
   tomatoes

Sour cream and chives
   (optional)

Shredded Cheddar
   cheese (optional)

*A highly seasoned Mexican
pork sausage.

1. Place beef and chorizo in **CROCK-POT**® slow cooker. Break up with fork to form small pieces. Stir beans and tomatoes into **CROCK-POT**® slow cooker.

2. Cover; cook on LOW 7 hours. Turn off heat. Let stand 10 to 12 minutes. Skim off excess fat from surface. Garnish with sour cream and chives. Serve with cheese, if desired.

Makes 6 servings

Roasted Tomato-Basil Soup

2 cans (28 ounces *each*) whole tomatoes, drained, 3 cups liquid reserved

2½ tablespoons packed dark brown sugar

1 medium onion, finely chopped

3 cups vegetable broth

3 tablespoons tomato paste

¼ teaspoon ground allspice

1 can (5 ounces) evaporated milk

¼ cup shredded fresh basil (about 10 large leaves)

Salt and black pepper

1. Preheat oven to 450°F. Line baking sheet with foil; spray with nonstick cooking spray. Arrange tomatoes on foil in single layer. Sprinkle with brown sugar; top with onion. Bake 25 minutes or until tomatoes look dry and light brown. Let tomatoes cool slightly; finely chop.

2. Place tomato mixture, 3 cups reserved liquid from tomatoes, broth, tomato paste and allspice in **CROCK-POT®** slow cooker; mix well. Cover; cook on LOW 8 hours or on HIGH 4 hours.

3. Add evaporated milk and basil; season with salt and pepper. Cover; cook on HIGH 30 minutes or until heated through.

Makes 6 servings

Simmered Split Pea Soup

(pictured on page 9)

3 cans (about 14 ounces *each*) chicken broth

1 package (16 ounces) dried split peas

8 slices bacon, crisp-cooked, chopped and divided

1 onion, chopped

2 carrots, chopped

1 teaspoon black pepper

½ teaspoon dried thyme

1 whole bay leaf

Combine broth, peas, half of bacon, onion, carrots, pepper, thyme and bay leaf in **CROCK-POT®** slow cooker. Cover; cook on LOW 6 to 8 hours. Remove and discard bay leaf. Garnish with remaining half of bacon.

Makes 6 servings

Roasted Tomato-Basil Soup

Black and White Chili

Nonstick cooking spray

1 pound boneless, skinless chicken breasts, cut into ¾-inch pieces

1 cup chopped onion

1 can (about 15 ounces) Great Northern beans, rinsed and drained

1 can (about 15 ounces) black beans, rinsed and drained

1 can (about 14 ounces) stewed tomatoes, undrained

2 tablespoons Texas-style chili seasoning mix

1. Spray large skillet with cooking spray; heat over medium heat. Add chicken and onion; cook and stir 5 minutes or until chicken is browned.

2. Combine chicken mixture, beans, tomatoes and chili seasoning in **CROCK-POT®** slow cooker. Cover; cook on LOW 4 to 4½ hours.

Makes 6 servings

Serving Suggestion: For a change of pace, this delicious chili is excellent served over cooked rice or pasta.

Potato Soup

(pictured on page 8)

8 slices smoked bacon, divided

1 large onion, chopped

2 stalks celery, chopped

2 carrots, chopped

3 cloves garlic, minced

1 teaspoon dried thyme

5 potatoes (about 3 pounds), cut into ½-inch cubes

4 cups chicken broth

1 cup half-and-half

Salt and black pepper

1. Heat large skillet over medium heat. Add bacon; cook and stir until crisp. Remove to paper towel-lined plate using slotted spoon; crumble.

2. Pour off all but 2 tablespoons bacon fat from skillet; return to medium-high heat. Add onion, celery, carrots, garlic and thyme; cook and stir 6 minutes. Stir onion mixture, potatoes, half of bacon and broth into **CROCK-POT®** slow cooker. Cover; cook on LOW 7 to 8 hours or on HIGH 3 to 4 hours.

3. Mash potatoes with potato masher and stir in half-and-half, salt and pepper. Cover; cook on HIGH 15 minutes. Garnish with remaining half of bacon.

Makes 8 servings

Black and White Chili

THE ORIGINAL SLOW COOKER

Broccoli Rabe and Sausage Rigatoni (page 54)

Turkey Stroganoff (page 53)

Pasta Dinners

Beefy Tortellini (page 52)

Three-Pepper Pasta Sauce

1 *each* red, yellow and green bell pepper, cut into 1-inch pieces

2 cans (about 14 ounces *each*) diced tomatoes

1 cup chopped onion

1 can (6 ounces) tomato paste

4 cloves garlic, minced

2 tablespoons olive oil

1 teaspoon dried basil

1 teaspoon dried oregano

½ teaspoon salt

¼ teaspoon red pepper flakes or black pepper

Hot cooked pasta

Grated Parmesan or Romano cheese

Combine bell peppers, tomatoes, onion, tomato paste, garlic, oil, basil, oregano, salt and red pepper flakes in **CROCK-POT®** slow cooker. Cover; cook on LOW 7 to 8 hours. Serve with pasta and cheese.

Makes 4 to 6 servings

 tip

Save preparation time! Substitute 3 cups of mixed bell pepper pieces from a salad bar for the bell peppers.

Spaghetti and Turkey Meatballs

1½ pounds ground turkey
½ cup seasoned dry bread crumbs
1 small onion, finely chopped
2 teaspoons garlic powder, divided
2 eggs
½ cup grated Parmesan cheese
½ teaspoon black pepper, divided
2 tablespoons olive oil
1 can (28 ounces) crushed tomatoes with basil, oregano and garlic
1 can (6 ounces) tomato paste
1 teaspoon dried basil
Hot cooked spaghetti
Chopped fresh Italian parsley (optional)

1. Coat inside of **CROCK-POT**® slow cooker with nonstick cooking spray. Combine turkey, bread crumbs, onion, 1 teaspoon garlic powder, eggs, cheese and ¼ teaspoon pepper in large bowl; mix well. Form mixture into 24 meatballs, about 1½ inches in diameter.

2. Heat oil in large skillet over medium-high heat. Add meatballs in batches; cook and stir 4 to 5 minutes or until browned on all sides. Remove meatballs to **CROCK-POT**® slow cooker using slotted spoon.

3. Combine tomatoes, tomato paste and basil in large bowl; stir to blend. Pour over meatballs. Cover; cook on LOW 6 to 7 hours or on HIGH 3 to 4 hours. Serve over spaghetti. Garnish with parsley.

Makes 6 servings

Artichoke Pasta

1 tablespoon olive oil

1 cup chopped sweet onion

4 cloves garlic, minced

1 can (28 ounces) crushed tomatoes

1 can (about 14 ounces) artichoke hearts, drained and cut into pieces

1 cup small pimiento-stuffed olives

¾ teaspoon red pepper flakes

8 ounces hot cooked fettuccine pasta

½ cup grated Asiago or Romano cheese

Fresh basil (optional)

1. Coat inside of **CROCK-POT®** slow cooker with nonstick cooking spray. Heat oil in small skillet over medium heat. Add onion; cook and stir 5 minutes. Add garlic; cook and stir 1 minute. Combine onion mixture, tomatoes, artichokes, olives and red pepper flakes in **CROCK-POT®** slow cooker.

2. Cover; cook on LOW 7 to 8 hours or on HIGH 3 to 4 hours. Top pasta with artichoke sauce and cheese. Garnish with basil.

Makes 4 servings

Stuffed Manicotti

1 container (15 ounces)
    ricotta cheese
1½ cups (6 ounces) shredded
    Italian cheese blend,
    divided
1 egg
¼ teaspoon ground nutmeg
10 uncooked manicotti shells
2 cans (about 14 ounces
    each) Italian seasoned
    stewed tomatoes
1 cup spicy marinara or
    tomato basil pasta
    sauce
  Chopped fresh basil
    or Italian parsley
    (optional)
  French bread (optional)

1. Combine ricotta cheese, 1 cup Italian cheese, egg and nutmeg in medium bowl; mix well. Spoon mixture into large resealable food storage bag; cut off small corner. Pipe cheese mixture into uncooked manicotti shells.

2. Coat inside of **CROCK-POT®** slow cooker with nonstick cooking spray. Combine tomatoes and pasta sauce in large bowl; stir until blended. Spoon 1½ cups sauce mixture into **CROCK-POT®** slow cooker. Arrange half of the stuffed shells in sauce. Repeat layering with 1½ cups sauce, remaining shells and remaining sauce. Cover; cook on LOW 2½ to 3 hours.

3. Sprinkle remaining ½ cup Italian cheese over top. Turn **CROCK-POT®** slow cooker to HIGH. Cover; cook on HIGH 10 to 15 minutes or until cheese is melted. Garnish with basil. Serve with bread, if desired.

Makes 5 servings

Garden Pasta

1 jar (24 to 26 ounces)
    puttanesca or spicy
    tomato basil pasta
    sauce
1 can (about 14 ounces)
    stewed tomatoes
1 cup small broccoli florets
1 cup finely diced yellow
    squash or zucchini *or*
    ½ cup *each*
½ cup water
2 cups (5 ounces) uncooked
    bowtie pasta
½ cup crumbled feta cheese
¼ cup chopped fresh basil

1. Coat inside of **CROCK-POT®** slow cooker with nonstick cooking spray. Combine pasta sauce, tomatoes, broccoli, squash, water and pasta in **CROCK-POT®** slow cooker; mix well.

2. Cover; cook on LOW 3½ to 4½ hours or on HIGH 2 to 2½ hours, stirring halfway through cooking time. Spoon into shallow bowls; top with cheese and basil.

Makes 4 to 6 servings

Pasta Shells with Prosciutto

3 cups (8 ounces) uncooked medium shell pasta

1 jar (24 to 26 ounces) vodka pasta sauce

¾ cup water

½ cup whipping cream

2 ounces (½ cup) torn or coarsely chopped thin sliced prosciutto

¼ cup chopped fresh chives

1. Coat inside of **CROCK-POT®** slow cooker with nonstick cooking spray. Combine pasta, pasta sauce and water in **CROCK-POT®** slow cooker. Cover; cook on LOW 2 hours or on HIGH 1 hour.

2. Stir in cream. Cover; cook on LOW 1 to 1½ hours or on HIGH 45 minutes to 1 hour or until pasta is tender.

3. Stir prosciutto into pasta mixture. Spoon into shallow bowls; top with chives.

Makes 4 servings

Easy Parmesan Chicken

8 ounces mushrooms, sliced

1 medium onion, cut into thin wedges

1 tablespoon olive oil

4 boneless, skinless chicken breasts

1 jar (26 ounces) pasta sauce

½ teaspoon dried basil

¼ teaspoon dried oregano

1 whole bay leaf

½ cup (2 ounces) shredded mozzarella cheese

¼ cup grated Parmesan cheese

Hot cooked spaghetti

1. Place mushrooms and onion in **CROCK-POT®** slow cooker.

2. Heat oil in large skillet over medium-high heat. Add chicken; cook 3 to 5 minutes on each side or until lightly browned. Place chicken in **CROCK-POT®** slow cooker. Pour pasta sauce over chicken; add basil, oregano and bay leaf. Cover; cook on LOW 6 to 7 hours or on HIGH 3 to 4 hours. Remove and discard bay leaf.

3. Sprinkle chicken with cheeses. Cook, uncovered, on LOW 10 minutes or until cheeses are melted. Serve over spaghetti.

Makes 4 servings

 tip

Dairy products should be added at the end of the cooking time because they will curdle if cooked in the **CROCK-POT®** slow cooker for a long time.

Vegetable Pasta Sauce

2 cans (about 14 ounces
   each) diced tomatoes
1 can (about 14 ounces)
   whole tomatoes,
   undrained
1½ cups sliced mushrooms
1 medium red bell pepper,
   diced
1 medium green bell
   pepper, diced
1 small yellow squash,
   cut into ¼-inch slices
1 small zucchini, cut into
   ¼-inch slices
1 can (6 ounces) tomato
   paste
4 green onions, sliced
2 tablespoons Italian
   seasoning
1 tablespoon chopped
   fresh Italian parsley
3 cloves garlic, minced
1 teaspoon salt
1 teaspoon red pepper
   flakes (optional)
1 teaspoon black pepper
   Hot cooked rigatoni pasta
   Grated Parmesan cheese
   (optional)

Combine tomatoes, mushrooms, bell peppers, squash, zucchini, tomato paste, green onions, Italian seasoning, parsley, garlic, salt, red pepper flakes, if desired, and black pepper in **CROCK-POT®** slow cooker; stir until well blended. Cover; cook on LOW 6 to 8 hours. Serve over pasta. Top with cheese, if desired.

Makes 4 to 6 servings

Cream Cheese Chicken with Broccoli

4 pounds boneless, skinless chicken breasts, cut into ½-inch pieces

1 tablespoon olive oil

1 package (1 ounce) Italian salad dressing mix

Nonstick cooking spray

2 cups (about 8 ounces) sliced mushrooms

1 cup chopped onion

1 can (10½ ounces) condensed cream of chicken soup, undiluted

1 bag (10 ounces) frozen broccoli florets, thawed

1 package (8 ounces) cream cheese, cubed

¼ cup dry sherry

Hot cooked pasta

1. Toss chicken with oil in large bowl. Sprinkle with salad dressing mix. Remove to **CROCK-POT®** slow cooker. Cover; cook on LOW 3 hours.

2. Spray large skillet with cooking spray; heat over medium heat. Add mushrooms and onion; cook 5 minutes or until onion is tender.

3. Add soup, broccoli, cream cheese and sherry to skillet; cook and stir until heated through. Remove to **CROCK-POT®** slow cooker. Cover; cook on LOW 1 hour. Serve chicken and sauce over pasta.

Makes 10 to 12 servings

 tip

For easier preparation, cut up the chicken and vegetables for this recipe the night before. Wrap the chicken and vegetables separately, and store in the refrigerator.

Beefy Tortellini

(pictured on page 33)

½ pound ground beef

1 jar (24 to 26 ounces) roasted tomato and garlic pasta sauce

½ cup water

8 ounces sliced button or exotic mushrooms, such as oyster, shiitake and cremini

½ teaspoon red pepper flakes (optional)

1 package (12 ounces) uncooked three-cheese tortellini

¾ cup grated Asiago or Romano cheese

Chopped fresh Italian parsley (optional)

1. Brown beef in large skillet over medium-high heat 6 to 8 minutes, stirring to break up meat. Drain fat.

2. Coat inside of **CROCK-POT®** slow cooker with nonstick cooking spray. Stir pasta sauce and water into **CROCK-POT®** slow cooker. Add mushrooms; stir to combine. Stir in meat, red pepper flakes, if desired, and tortellini. Cover; cook on LOW 2 hours or on HIGH 1 hour. Stir.

3. Cover; cook on LOW 2 to 2½ hours or on HIGH ½ to 1 hour. Serve in shallow bowls topped with cheese and parsley, if desired.

Makes 6 servings

Turkey Stroganoff

(pictured on page 32)

Nonstick cooking spray

4 cups sliced mushrooms

2 stalks celery, thinly sliced

**2 medium shallots *or*
½ small onion, minced**

1 cup chicken broth

½ teaspoon dried thyme

¼ teaspoon black pepper

**2 turkey tenderloins, turkey
breasts *or* boneless,
skinless chicken thighs
(about 10 ounces *each*),
cut into 1-inch pieces**

½ cup sour cream

**1 tablespoon plus
1 teaspoon all-
purpose flour**

¼ teaspoon salt

**1⅓ cups hot cooked wide
egg noodles**

1. Spray large skillet with nonstick cooking spray; heat over medium heat. Add mushrooms, celery and shallots; cook and stir 5 minutes or until mushrooms and shallot are tender. Spoon into **CROCK-POT®** slow cooker. Stir broth, thyme and pepper into **CROCK-POT®** slow cooker. Stir in turkey. Cover; cook on LOW 5 to 6 hours.

2. Mix sour cream into flour in small bowl. Spoon 2 tablespoons liquid from **CROCK-POT®** slow cooker into sour cream mixture; stir well. Stir sour cream mixture into **CROCK-POT®** slow cooker. Cover; cook on LOW 10 minutes.

3. Season with salt. Spoon noodles onto each plate to serve. Top with turkey mixture.

Makes 4 servings

Ham and Cheese Pasta Bake

12 ounces uncooked rigatoni
    pasta
1 ham steak, cubed
1 container (10 ounces)
    refrigerated Alfredo
    sauce
2 cups (8 ounces) shredded
    mozzarella cheese,
    divided
2 cups half-and-half,
    warmed
1 tablespoon cornstarch

1. Fill large saucepan with salted water; bring to a boil over high heat. Add pasta; cook 7 minutes. Drain pasta; remove to **CROCK-POT®** slow cooker.

2. Stir ham, Alfredo sauce and 1 cup cheese into pasta. Stir half-and-half into cornstarch in medium bowl until smooth; pour over pasta. Sprinkle with remaining 1 cup cheese. Cover; cook on LOW 3½ to 4 hours or until pasta is tender and liquid is absorbed.

Makes 6 servings

Broccoli Rabe and Sausage Rigatoni

(pictured on page 32)

2 tablespoons olive oil
3 sweet or hot Italian
    sausage links,
    casings removed
2 cloves garlic, minced
1 large bunch (about
    1¼ pounds) broccoli
    rabe, trimmed and cut
    into 1-inch lengths
½ cup chicken broth
½ teaspoon salt
½ teaspoon red pepper
    flakes
1 pound hot cooked
    rigatoni pasta
    Grated Parmesan cheese
    (optional)

1. Coat inside of **CROCK-POT®** slow cooker with nonstick cooking spray. Heat oil in large skillet over medium heat. Add sausage; cook and stir 6 to 8 minutes or until browned. Add garlic; cook and stir 1 minute or until softened and fragrant. Remove to **CROCK-POT®** slow cooker using slotted spoon.

2. Add broccoli rabe to **CROCK-POT®** slow cooker with sausage. Pour in broth; season with salt and red pepper flakes. Cover; cook on LOW 4 hours or on HIGH 2 hours.

3. Stir pasta into sausage mixture in **CROCK-POT®** slow cooker just before serving. Garnish with cheese.

Makes 6 servings

Ham and Cheese Pasta Bake

· THE ORIGINAL SLOW COOKER ·

Easy Family Burritos (page 78)

Cinnamon Roll and Sweet 'Tater Gratin (page 67)

Kids' Favorites

Super Meatball Sliders (page 66)

Pulled Pork Sliders
with Cola Barbecue Sauce

1 teaspoon vegetable oil

3 pounds boneless pork shoulder roast, cut evenly into 4 pieces

1 cup cola

¼ cup tomato paste

2 tablespoons packed brown sugar

2 teaspoons Worcestershire sauce

2 teaspoons spicy brown mustard

Hot pepper sauce

Salt

16 dinner rolls or potato rolls, split

Sliced pickles (optional)

1. Heat oil in large skillet over medium-high heat. Brown pork on all sides. Remove to **CROCK-POT®** slow cooker. Pour cola over pork. Cover; cook on LOW 7½ to 8 hours or on HIGH 3½ to 4 hours.

2. Remove pork to cutting board. Cover loosely with foil; let stand 10 to 15 minutes. Shred pork with two forks.

3. Skim fat from cooking liquid. Whisk tomato paste, brown sugar, Worcestershire sauce and mustard into **CROCK-POT®** slow cooker. Cover; cook on HIGH 15 minutes or until thickened.

4. Stir shredded pork into **CROCK-POT®** slow cooker. Season with hot pepper sauce and salt. Serve on rolls. Top with pickles, if desired.

Makes 16 sliders

Southwest-Style Meat Loaf

1½ pounds ground beef

2 eggs

1 small onion, chopped (about ½ cup)

½ medium green bell pepper, chopped (about ½ cup)

½ cup plain dry bread crumbs

¾ cup chunky salsa, divided

1½ teaspoons ground cumin

¾ cup (3 ounces) shredded Mexican cheese blend

¾ teaspoon salt

¼ teaspoon black pepper

1. Combine beef, eggs, onion, bell pepper, bread crumbs, ¼ cup salsa, cumin, cheese, salt and black pepper in large bowl; mix well. Form mixture into 9×5-inch loaf.

2. Fold two long pieces of foil in half lengthwise. (Each should be about 24 inches long.) Crisscross pieces on work surface, coat with nonstick cooking spray and set meat loaf on top. Use ends of foil as handles to gently lower meat loaf into **CROCK-POT®** slow cooker, letting ends hang over the top. Top meat loaf with remaining ½ cup salsa.

3. Cover; cook on LOW 7 to 8 hours or on HIGH 3 to 4 hours or until meat loaf is firm and cooked through. Remove meat loaf to cutting board; let stand 5 minutes before slicing.

Makes 6 servings

Tuna Casserole

2 cans (10¾ ounces *each*)
 cream of celery soup
2 cans (5 ounces *each*) tuna
 in water, drained and
 flaked
1 cup water
2 carrots, chopped
1 small red onion, chopped
¼ teaspoon black pepper
1 egg
8 ounces hot cooked egg
 noodles
 Plain dry bread crumbs
2 tablespoons chopped
 fresh Italian parsley

1. Stir soup, tuna, water, carrots, onion and pepper into **CROCK-POT®** slow cooker. Place whole unpeeled egg on top. Cover; cook on LOW 4 to 5 hours or on HIGH 1½ to 3 hours.

2. Remove egg; stir in pasta. Cover; cook on HIGH ½ to 1 hour or until onion is tender. Meanwhile, mash egg in small bowl; mix in bread crumbs and parsley. Top casserole with bread crumb mixture.

Makes 6 servings

Note: This casserole calls for a raw egg. The egg will hard-cook in its shell in the **CROCK-POT®** slow cooker.

Quick and Easy Homemade Chicken and Dumplings

1 whole chicken (3 to 5 pounds), cut into pieces

2 large potatoes, cubed

3 medium carrots, chopped

1 cup chopped celery

4 tablespoons Italian seasoning, divided

1 whole bay leaf

1½ cups milk, divided

3 cups all-purpose flour, divided

3 tablespoons butter

½ teaspoon baking soda

Salt and black pepper

1. Coat inside of **CROCK-POT®** slow cooker with nonstick cooking spray. Combine chicken, potatoes, carrots, celery, 3 tablespoons Italian seasoning and bay leaf in **CROCK-POT®** slow cooker; add enough water to cover chicken. Cover; cook on HIGH 4 hours.

2. Remove chicken to cutting board; shred with two forks. Stir ½ cup milk into 1 cup flour in small bowl until smooth. Whisk flour mixture into **CROCK-POT®** slow cooker; add shredded chicken.

3. Combine remaining 2 cups flour, butter, remaining 1 tablespoon Italian seasoning, baking soda, salt and pepper in medium bowl. Stir in remaining 1 cup milk to form soft dough. Drop dough by tablespoonfuls onto top of chicken mixture in **CROCK-POT®** slow cooker. Turn **CROCK-POT®** slow cooker to LOW. Cover; cook on LOW 30 minutes or until dumplings are cooked through. Remove and discard bay leaf.

Makes 10 to 12 servings

Super Meatball Sliders

(pictured on page 57)

1 can (15 ounces) whole berry cranberry sauce

1 can (about 15 ounces) tomato sauce

⅛ teaspoon red pepper flakes (optional)

2 pounds ground beef or turkey

¾ cup dry seasoned bread crumbs

1 egg, lightly beaten

1 package (1 ounce) dry onion soup mix

Nonstick cooking spray

Baby arugula leaves (optional)

24 small potato rolls or dinner rolls, split

6 slices (1 ounce *each*) provolone cheese, cut into quarters

1. Combine cranberry sauce, tomato sauce and red pepper flakes, if desired, in **CROCK-POT®** slow cooker. Cover; cook on LOW 3 to 4 hours.

2. Halfway through cooking time, prepare meatballs. Combine beef, bread crumbs, egg and soup mix in large bowl; mix well. Shape mixture into 24 meatballs (about 1¾ inches diameter). Spray medium skillet with cooking spray; heat over medium heat. Add meatballs; cook 8 to 10 minutes or until well browned on all sides. Remove meatballs to **CROCK-POT®** slow cooker.

3. Cover; cook on LOW 1 to 2 hours or until meatballs are no longer pink in centers. Place arugula leaves on bottom of rolls, if desired; top with meatballs and cheese. Spoon sauce over meatballs; cover with tops of rolls.

Makes 24 sliders

Cinnamon Roll and Sweet 'Tater Gratin

(pictured on page 56)

3 pounds sweet potatoes, cut into ¼-inch thick rounds

¾ cup (3 ounces) shredded mozzarella cheese

1 cup whipping cream

¼ to ½ teaspoon ground red pepper

Salt and black pepper

4 tablespoons (½ stick) butter, divided

1 can (about 12 ounces) refrigerated cinnamon roll dough

1. Coat inside of **CROCK-POT®** slow cooker with nonstick cooking spray. Arrange one third of sweet potatoes in **CROCK-POT®** slow cooker, overlapping slightly. Top with ¼ cup cheese. Repeat layers two additional times using sweet potatoes and cheese.

2. Combine cream, ground red pepper, salt and black pepper in small bowl; mix well. Pour cream mixture over sweet potato layers in **CROCK-POT®** slow cooker. Dot with 2 tablespoons butter.

3. Remove cinnamon roll dough from can; unroll into long strips. Set aside icing. Arrange strips of dough in lattice design on top of sweet potato layers, making sure edges are sealed. Dot dough with remaining 2 tablespoons butter. Cover; cook on HIGH 4 hours.

4. Turn off heat. Drizzle gratin with reserved icing. Let stand, uncovered, 15 minutes before serving.

Makes 10 servings

Vegetable-Stuffed Pork Chops

4 bone-in pork chops
  Salt and black pepper
1 can (about 15 ounces) corn, drained
1 green bell pepper, chopped
1 cup seasoned dry bread crumbs
1 small onion, chopped
½ cup uncooked converted long grain rice
1 can (8 ounces) tomato sauce

1. Cut pocket into each pork chop, cutting from edge to bone. Lightly season pockets with salt and black pepper. Combine corn, bell pepper, bread crumbs, onion and rice in large bowl. Stuff pork chops with rice mixture. Secure open side with toothpicks.

2. Place any remaining rice mixture in **CROCK-POT®** slow cooker; top with stuffed pork chops. Pour tomato sauce over pork chops. Cover; cook on LOW 8 to 10 hours.

3. Remove pork chops to serving platter. Remove and discard toothpicks. Serve with extra rice mixture.

Makes 4 servings

tip

Your butcher can cut a pocket in the pork chops to save you time and to ensure even cooking.

Ravioli Casserole

8 ounces pork or turkey
  Italian sausage,
  casings removed

½ cup minced onion

1½ cups marinara sauce

1 can (about 14 ounces)
  Italian-style diced
  tomatoes

2 packages (9 ounces *each*)
  refrigerated meatless
  ravioli, such as wild
  mushroom or three
  cheese, divided

1½ cups (6 ounces) shredded
  mozzarella cheese,
  divided

Chopped fresh Italian
  parsley (optional)

1. Heat large skillet over medium-high heat. Brown sausage and onion 6 to 8 minutes, stirring to break up meat. Drain fat. Stir in marinara sauce and tomatoes; mix well. Remove from heat.

2. Coat inside of **CROCK-POT®** slow cooker with nonstick cooking spray. Spoon 1 cup sauce into **CROCK-POT®** slow cooker. Layer half of 1 package of ravioli over sauce; top with additional ½ cup sauce. Repeat layering once; top with ½ cup cheese. Repeat layering with remaining package ravioli and all remaining sauce, reserve remaining ½ cup cheese. Cover; cook on LOW 2½ to 3 hours or on HIGH 1½ to 2 hours or until sauce is heated through and ravioli is tender.

3. Sprinkle remaining ½ cup cheese over top of casserole. Cover; cook on HIGH 15 minutes or until cheese is melted. Garnish with parsley.

Makes 4 to 6 servings

Red Beans and Rice

2 cans (about 15 ounces *each*) red beans, undrained

1 can (about 14 ounces) diced tomatoes

½ cup chopped celery

½ cup chopped green bell pepper

½ cup chopped green onions

2 cloves garlic, minced

1 to 2 teaspoons hot pepper sauce

1 teaspoon Worcestershire sauce

1 whole bay leaf

3 cups hot cooked rice

1. Combine beans, tomatoes, celery, bell pepper, green onions, garlic, hot pepper sauce, Worcestershire sauce and bay leaf in **CROCK-POT®** slow cooker; stir to blend. Cover; cook on LOW 4 to 6 hours or on HIGH 2 to 3 hours.

2. Mash bean mixture slightly in **CROCK-POT®** slow cooker until mixture thickens. Cover; cook on HIGH ½ to 1 hour. Remove and discard bay leaf. Serve bean mixture over rice.

Makes 6 servings

Simple Barbecue Chicken

1 bottle (20 ounces)
    ketchup
⅔ cup packed brown sugar
⅔ cup cider vinegar
2 tablespoons chili powder
2 tablespoons tomato paste
1 tablespoon onion powder
2 teaspoons garlic powder
2 teaspoons liquid smoke
    (optional)
1 teaspoon hot pepper
    sauce (optional)
8 boneless, skinless
    chicken breasts
    (6 ounces *each*)
8 whole wheat rolls

1. Combine ketchup, brown sugar, vinegar, chili powder, tomato paste, onion powder, garlic powder, liquid smoke and hot pepper sauce, if desired, in **CROCK-POT**® slow cooker.

2. Add chicken. Cover; cook on LOW 4 to 6 hours or on HIGH 2 to 3 hours or until chicken is cooked through. Serve with rolls.

Makes 8 servings

Pulled Chicken Sandwiches: Shred the chicken and serve on whole wheat rolls or hamburger buns. Top with mixed greens or coleslaw.

Slow Cooker Pizza Casserole

1½ pounds ground beef

1 pound bulk pork sausage

4 jars (14 ounces *each*) pizza sauce

2 cups (8 ounces) shredded mozzarella cheese

2 cups grated Parmesan cheese

2 cans (4 ounces *each*) mushroom stems and pieces, drained

2 packages (3 ounces *each*) sliced pepperoni

½ cup finely chopped onion

½ cup finely chopped green bell pepper

1 clove garlic, minced

1 pound corkscrew pasta, cooked and drained

1. Brown beef and sausage in large nonstick skillet over medium-high heat 6 to 8 minutes, stirring to break up meat. Drain fat. Remove beef mixture to **CROCK-POT**® slow cooker.

2. Add pizza sauce, cheeses, mushrooms, pepperoni, onion, bell pepper and garlic; stir to blend. Cover; cook on LOW 3½ hours or on HIGH 2 hours.

3. Stir in pasta. Cover; cook on HIGH 15 to 20 minutes or until pasta is heated through.

Makes 6 servings

Ham and Potato Casserole

1½ pounds red potatoes,
    unpeeled and sliced
8 ounces thinly sliced deli
    ham
2 poblano chile peppers,
    cut into thin slices
2 tablespoons olive oil
1 tablespoon dried oregano
¼ teaspoon salt
1 cup (4 ounces) shredded
    Monterey Jack cheese
2 tablespoons finely
    chopped fresh cilantro

1. Combine potatoes, ham, chile peppers, oil, oregano and salt in **CROCK-POT®** slow cooker; stir to blend. Cover; cook on LOW 7 hours or on HIGH 4 hours.

2. Remove potato mixture to large serving platter. Sprinkle with cheese and cilantro; let stand 3 minutes or until cheese is melted.

Makes 6 servings

Easy Family Burritos

(pictured on page 56)

1 boneless beef chuck
    shoulder roast
    (2 to 3 pounds)*
1 jar (24 ounces) *or* 2 jars
    (16 ounces *each*) salsa
Flour tortillas, warmed
Optional toppings:
    shredded lettuce,
    diced tomato and/or
    diced onion

*Unless you have a 5-, 6- or 7-quart **CROCK-POT®** slow cooker, cut any roast larger than 2½ pounds in half so it cooks completely.*

1. Place beef in **CROCK-POT®** slow cooker; top with salsa. Cover; cook on LOW 8 to 10 hours.

2. Remove beef to cutting board; shred with two forks. Return to cooking liquid; mix well. Cover; cook on LOW 1 to 2 hours or until heated through. Serve in tortillas. Top as desired.

Makes 8 servings

Ham and Potato Casserole

Chunky Ranch Potatoes (page 104)   French Carrot Medley (page 90)

Satisfying Sides

Corn on the Cob with Garlic Herb Butter (page 90)

Sunshine Squash

1 butternut squash (about 2 pounds), seeded and diced

1 can (about 15 ounces) corn, drained

1 can (about 14 ounces) diced tomatoes

1 onion, coarsely chopped

1 green bell pepper, cut into 1-inch pieces

½ cup chicken broth

1 mild green chile, coarsely chopped

1 clove garlic, minced

½ teaspoon salt

¼ teaspoon black pepper

1 tablespoon plus 1½ teaspoons tomato paste

1. Combine squash, corn, diced tomatoes, onion, bell pepper, broth, green chile, garlic, salt and black pepper in **CROCK-POT®** slow cooker. Cover; cook on LOW 6 hours.

2. Remove about ¼ cup cooking liquid; blend liquid with tomato paste in small bowl. Stir mixture into **CROCK-POT®** slow cooker. Cover; cook on LOW 30 minutes or until mixture is slightly thickened and heated through.

Makes 6 to 8 servings

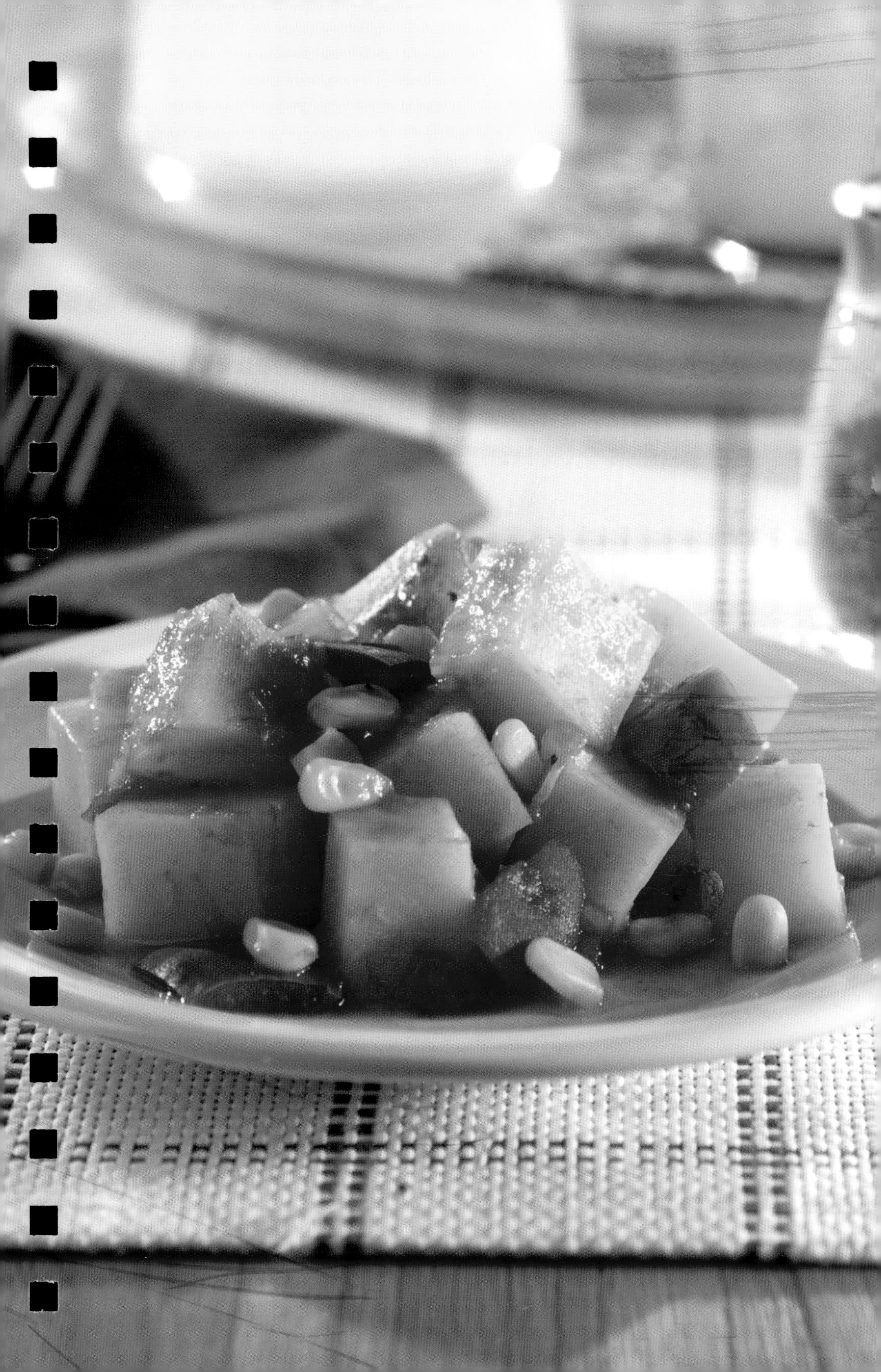

Cauliflower Mash

**2 heads cauliflower
(8 cups florets)**
1 tablespoon butter
**1 tablespoon half-and-half
or whole milk**
Salt
**Sprigs fresh Italian
parsley (optional)**

1. Arrange cauliflower in **CROCK-POT®** slow cooker; add enough water to fill **CROCK-POT®** slow cooker about 2 inches. Cover; cook on LOW 5 to 6 hours. Drain well.

2. Place cooked cauliflower in food processor or blender; process until almost smooth. Add butter; process until smooth. Add half-and-half as needed to reach desired consistency. Season with salt. Garnish with parsley.

Makes 6 servings

tip

You may substitute the same amount of cream, buttermilk or chicken broth for the half-and-half.

Candied Sweet Potatoes

3 medium sweet potatoes
(1½ to 2 pounds),
sliced into ½-inch
rounds

½ cup water

¼ cup (½ stick) butter, cut
into pieces

¼ cup plus 2 tablespoons
sugar

1 tablespoon vanilla

1 teaspoon nutmeg

Combine sweet potatoes, water, butter, sugar, vanilla and nutmeg in **CROCK-POT®** slow cooker; mix well. Cover; cook on LOW 7 hours or on HIGH 4 hours.

Makes 4 servings

Red Cabbage and Apples

1 small head red cabbage,
cored and thinly sliced

1 large apple, peeled and
grated

¾ cup sugar

½ cup red wine vinegar

1 teaspoon ground cloves

½ cup bacon, crisp-cooked
and crumbled

Fresh apple slices
(optional)

Combine cabbage, grated apples, sugar, vinegar and cloves in **CROCK-POT®** slow cooker. Cover; cook on HIGH 6 hours, stirring halfway through cooking time. Sprinkle with bacon. Garnish with apple slices.

Makes 6 servings

Candied Sweet Potatoes

Buttery Vegetable Gratin

3 leeks, halved lengthwise and cut into 1-inch pieces

1 red bell pepper, cut into ½-inch pieces

5 tablespoons unsalted butter, divided

4 tablespoons grated Parmesan cheese, divided

1 teaspoon fresh thyme, divided

¾ teaspoon salt, divided

¼ plus ⅛ teaspoon black pepper, divided

2 zucchini (about 1½ pounds total), cut into ¾-inch-thick slices

2 yellow squash (about 1½ pounds total), cut into ¾-inch-thick slices

1½ cups fresh bread crumbs

1. Coat inside of **CROCK-POT®** slow cooker with nonstick cooking spray. Place leeks and bell pepper in bottom of **CROCK-POT®** slow cooker. Dot with 1 tablespoon butter, 1 tablespoon cheese, ½ teaspoon thyme, ¼ teaspoon salt and ⅛ teaspoon black pepper.

2. Arrange zucchini in single layer over leeks, overlapping as necessary. Dot with 1 tablespoon butter, 1 tablespoon cheese, remaining ½ teaspoon thyme, ¼ teaspoon salt and ⅛ teaspoon black pepper.

3. Arrange yellow squash in single layer over zucchini, overlapping as necessary. Dot with 1 tablespoon butter, remaining 2 tablespoons cheese, ¼ teaspoon salt and ⅛ teaspoon black pepper. Cover; cook on LOW 4 to 5 hours or until vegetables are soft.

4. Meanwhile, melt remaining 2 tablespoons butter in large skillet over medium-high heat. Add bread crumbs; cook and stir 6 minutes or until crisp and golden brown. Remove to medium bowl; set aside to cool. Sprinkle over vegetable mixture just before serving.

Makes 12 servings

Corn on the Cob with Garlic Herb Butter

(pictured on page 81)

4 to 5 ears of corn, husked
½ cup (1 stick) unsalted butter, softened
3 to 4 cloves garlic, minced
2 tablespoons finely minced fresh Italian parsley
Salt and black pepper

1. Place each ear of corn on a piece of foil. Combine butter, garlic and parsley in small bowl; spread onto corn. Season with salt and pepper; tightly seal foil.

2. Place in **CROCK-POT®** slow cooker, overlapping ears, if necessary. Add enough water to come one fourth of the way up each ear. Cover; cook on LOW 4 to 5 hours or on HIGH 2 to 2½ hours.

Makes 4 to 5 servings

French Carrot Medley

(pictured on page 80)

2 cups sliced carrots
¾ cup unsweetened orange juice
1 can (4 ounces) sliced mushrooms, undrained
4 stalks celery, sliced
2 tablespoons chopped onion
½ teaspoon dried dill weed
Salt and black pepper
¼ cup cold water
2 teaspoons cornstarch

1. Combine carrots, orange juice, mushrooms, celery, onion, dill weed, salt and pepper in **CROCK-POT®** slow cooker. Cover; cook on LOW 3 to 4 hours or on HIGH 2 hours.

2. Stir water into cornstarch in small bowl until smooth. Whisk into cooking liquid in **CROCK-POT®** slow cooker. Cover; cook on HIGH 15 minutes or until sauce is thickened. Spoon sauce over vegetable mixture before serving.

Makes 6 servings

Chili Barbecue Beans

1 cup dried **Great Northern beans, rinsed and sorted**

1 cup dried **red beans or dried kidney beans, rinsed and sorted**

1 cup dried **baby lima beans, rinsed and sorted**

3 cups **water**

8 slices **bacon, crisp-cooked and crumbled** *or* 8 ounces **smoked sausage, sliced**

¼ cup **packed brown sugar**

2 tablespoons **minced onion**

2 cubes **beef bouillon**

1 teaspoon **dry mustard**

1 teaspoon **chili powder**

1 teaspoon **minced garlic**

½ teaspoon **black pepper**

¼ teaspoon **red pepper flakes**

2 whole **bay leaves**

1 to 1½ cups **barbecue sauce**

1. Place beans in large bowl and add enough cold water to cover by at least 2 inches. Soak 6 to 8 hours or overnight.* Drain beans; discard water.

2. Combine soaked beans, 3 cups water, bacon, brown sugar, onion, bouillon cubes, mustard, chili powder, garlic, black pepper, red pepper flakes and bay leaves in **CROCK-POT®** slow cooker. Cover; cook on LOW 8 to 10 hours.

3. Stir in barbecue sauce. Cover; cook on LOW 1 hour or until heated through. Remove and discard bay leaves. Serve warm.

To quick soak beans, place beans in large saucepan and cover with water. Bring to a boil over high heat. Boil 2 minutes. Remove from heat; let soak, covered, 1 hour.

Makes 8 to 10 servings

Cran-Orange Acorn Squash

5 tablespoons instant brown rice

3 tablespoons minced onion

3 tablespoons diced celery

3 tablespoons dried cranberries

Pinch ground sage

3 small acorn or carnival squash, cut in half

1 teaspoon butter, cut into cubes

3 tablespoons orange juice

½ cup warm water

1. Combine rice, onion, celery, cranberries and sage in small bowl. Stuff each squash with rice mixture; dot with butter. Pour ½ tablespoon orange juice into each squash half over stuffing.

2. Stand squash in **CROCK-POT®** slow cooker. Pour water into **CROCK-POT®** slow cooker. Cover; cook on LOW 2½ hours or until squash is tender.

Makes 6 servings

Green Bean Casserole

2 packages (10 ounces *each*) frozen green beans, thawed

1 can (10½ ounces) condensed cream of mushroom soup, undiluted

1 tablespoon chopped fresh Italian parsley

1 tablespoon chopped roasted red peppers

1 teaspoon dried sage

½ teaspoon salt

½ teaspoon black pepper

¼ teaspoon ground nutmeg

½ cup toasted slivered almonds*

*To toast almonds, spread in single layer in heavy skillet. Cook over medium heat 1 to 2 minutes or until nuts are lightly browned, stirring frequently.

Combine green beans, soup, parsley, red peppers, sage, salt, black pepper and nutmeg in **CROCK-POT**® slow cooker. Cover; cook on LOW 3 to 4 hours. Sprinkle with almonds just before serving.

Makes 4 to 6 servings

Parmesan Potato Wedges

**2 pounds red potatoes,
  unpeeled and cut into
  ½-inch wedges**
**¼ cup finely chopped yellow
  onion**
1½ teaspoons dried oregano
½ teaspoon salt
¼ teaspoon black pepper
2 tablespoons butter, cubed
**¼ cup grated Parmesan
  cheese**

1. Layer potatoes, onion, oregano, salt and pepper in **CROCK-POT®** slow cooker; dot with butter. Cover; cook on HIGH 4 hours.

2. Remove potatoes to serving platter; sprinkle with cheese.

Makes 6 servings

 tip

Freshly grated Parmesan cheese will have a much better flavor and texture than the canned versions.

Slow-Cooked Succotash

2 teaspoons canola oil

1 cup diced onion

1 cup diced green bell
   pepper

1 cup diced celery

1 teaspoon paprika

1½ cups frozen corn, thawed

1½ cups frozen lima beans,
   thawed

1 cup canned diced
   tomatoes

2 teaspoons dried parsley
   flakes *or* 1 tablespoon
   minced fresh Italian
   parsley

½ teaspoon salt

½ teaspoon black pepper

1. Heat oil in large skillet over medium heat. Add onion, bell pepper and celery; cook and stir 5 minutes or until onion is translucent and bell pepper and celery are crisp-tender. Stir in paprika.

2. Combine onion mixture, corn, beans, tomatoes, parsley, salt and black pepper in **CROCK-POT®** slow cooker; stir to blend. Cover; cook on LOW 6 to 8 hours or on HIGH 3 to 4 hours.

Makes 8 servings

Escalloped Corn

2 tablespoons butter
½ cup chopped onion
3 tablespoons all-purpose
 flour
1 cup milk
4 cups frozen corn, thawed
 and divided
½ teaspoon salt
½ teaspoon dried thyme
¼ teaspoon black pepper
⅛ teaspoon ground nutmeg
 Sprigs fresh thyme
 (optional)

1. Melt butter in medium saucepan over medium heat. Add onion; cook and stir 5 minutes or until tender. Add flour; cook and stir 1 minute. Stir in milk. Bring to a boil; cook and stir 1 minute or until thickened.

2. Process 2 cups corn in food processor or blender until coarsely chopped. Combine milk mixture, chopped and remaining whole corn, salt, dried thyme, pepper and nutmeg in **CROCK-POT**® slow cooker; stir to blend. Cover; cook on LOW 3½ to 4 hours or until mixture is bubbly around edge. Garnish with fresh thyme.

Makes 6 servings

tip

Always taste your dish before serving and adjust the seasonings, including salt and pepper.

Cheesy Cauliflower

3 pounds cauliflower florets

¼ cup water

5 tablespoons unsalted butter

1 cup finely chopped onion

6 tablespoons all-purpose flour

¼ teaspoon dry mustard

2 cups milk

2 cups (8 ounces) shredded sharp Cheddar cheese

Salt and black pepper

1. Coat inside of **CROCK-POT®** slow cooker with nonstick cooking spray. Add cauliflower and water.

2. Melt butter in medium saucepan over medium-high heat. Add onion; cook 4 to 5 minutes or until slightly softened. Add flour and mustard; cook and stir 3 minutes or until well combined. Whisk in milk until smooth. Bring to a boil; cook 1 to 2 minutes or until thickened. Stir in cheese, salt and pepper. Cook and stir until cheese is melted.

3. Pour cheese mixture into **CROCK-POT®** slow cooker. Cover; cook on LOW 4 to 4½ hours.

Makes 8 to 10 servings

Coconut-Lime Sweet Potatoes

2½ pounds sweet potatoes, cut into 1-inch pieces

8 ounces shredded carrots

¾ cup shredded coconut, divided

1 tablespoon unsalted butter, melted

3 tablespoons sugar

½ teaspoon salt

⅓ cup walnuts, toasted, coarsely chopped and divided*

2 teaspoons grated lime peel

1. Combine sweet potatoes, carrots, ½ cup coconut, butter, sugar and salt in **CROCK-POT®** slow cooker. Cover; cook on LOW 5 to 6 hours. Remove to large bowl.

2. Mash sweet potatoes with potato masher. Stir in 3 tablespoons walnuts and lime peel. Sprinkle with remaining walnuts and ¼ cup coconut.

Makes 8 servings

*To toast walnuts, spread in single layer in small skillet. Cook and stir over medium heat 1 to 2 minutes or until lightly browned.

Cheesy Cauliflower

Slow-Good Apples and Carrots

6 carrots, sliced into ½-inch slices

4 apples, peeled, cored and sliced

¼ cup plus 1 tablespoon all-purpose flour

1 tablespoon packed brown sugar

½ teaspoon ground nutmeg

1 tablespoon butter, cubed

½ cup orange juice

Layer carrots and apples in **CROCK-POT®** slow cooker. Combine flour, brown sugar and nutmeg in small bowl; sprinkle over carrots and apples. Dot with butter; pour in juice. Cover; cook on LOW 3½ to 4 hours or until carrots are crisp-tender.

Makes 6 servings

Chunky Ranch Potatoes

(pictured on page 80)

3 pounds unpeeled red potatoes, quartered

1 cup water

½ cup prepared ranch dressing

½ cup grated Parmesan or Cheddar cheese

¼ cup minced fresh chives

1. Place potatoes in **CROCK-POT®** slow cooker. Add water. Cover; cook on LOW 7 to 9 hours or on HIGH 4 to 6 hours.

2. Stir in ranch dressing, cheese and chives. Break up potatoes into large pieces.

Makes 8 servings

Slow-Good Apples and Carrots

Cherry Delight (page 116)

Fruit and Nut Baked Apples (page 113)

Delicious Desserts

Fudge and Cream Pudding Cake (page 118)

Peach Cobbler

2 packages (16 ounces *each*) frozen peaches, thawed and drained

½ cup plus 1 tablespoon sugar, divided

2 teaspoons ground cinnamon, divided

½ teaspoon ground nutmeg

¾ cup all-purpose flour

6 tablespoons butter, cubed

Whipped cream (optional)

1. Combine peaches, ½ cup sugar, 1½ teaspoons cinnamon and nutmeg in **CROCK-POT**® slow cooker; stir to blend.

2. Combine flour, remaining 1 tablespoon sugar and remaining ½ teaspoon cinnamon in small bowl. Cut in butter with pastry blender or two knives until mixture resembles coarse crumbs. Sprinkle over peach mixture. Cover; cook on HIGH 2 hours. Serve with whipped cream, if desired.

Makes 4 to 6 servings

 tip

To make cleanup easier when cooking sticky or sugary foods, spray the inside of the **CROCK-POT**® slow cooker with nonstick cooking spray before adding ingredients.

S'mores Fondue

4 ounces semisweet
    chocolate chips
½ jar (about 3 ounces)
    marshmallow creme
3 tablespoons half-and-half
½ teaspoon vanilla
½ cup mini marshmallows
    Bananas, strawberries,
    chocolate-covered
    pretzels, graham
    crackers and/or sliced
    apples

1. Combine chocolate chips, marshmallow creme and half-and-half in medium saucepan. Cook over medium heat 2 minutes or until melted and smooth, stirring constantly. Remove from heat. Stir in vanilla.

2. Coat inside of **CROCK-POT® LITTLE DIPPER®** slow cooker with nonstick cooking spray. Fill with warm fondue. Sprinkle with marshmallows and serve with fruit, pretzels and graham crackers.

Makes 1½ cups

Bananas Foster

12 bananas, cut into quarters
1 cup flaked coconut
1 cup dark corn syrup
⅔ cup butter, melted
¼ cup lemon juice
2 teaspoons grated lemon
    peel
2 teaspoons rum
1 teaspoon ground
    cinnamon
½ teaspoon salt
12 slices pound cake
1 quart vanilla ice cream

1. Combine bananas and coconut in **CROCK-POT®** slow cooker. Stir corn syrup, butter, lemon juice, lemon peel, rum, cinnamon and salt in medium bowl; pour over bananas.

2. Cover; cook on LOW 1 to 2 hours. To serve, arrange bananas on pound cake. Top with ice cream and warm sauce.

Makes 12 servings

S'mores Fondue

Pumpkin Custard

1 cup solid-pack pumpkin
½ cup packed brown sugar
2 eggs, beaten
½ teaspoon ground ginger
½ teaspoon grated lemon
   peel
½ teaspoon ground
   cinnamon, plus
   additional for garnish
1 can (12 ounces)
   evaporated milk

1. Combine pumpkin, brown sugar, eggs, ginger, lemon peel and ½ teaspoon cinnamon in large bowl. Stir in evaporated milk. Divide mixture among six ramekins or custard cups. Cover each cup tightly with foil.

2. Place ramekins in **CROCK-POT**® slow cooker. Pour water into **CROCK-POT**® slow cooker to come about ½ inch from top of ramekins. Cover; cook on LOW 4 hours.

3. Use tongs or slotted spoon to remove ramekins from **CROCK-POT**® slow cooker. Sprinkle with additional ground cinnamon. Serve warm.

Makes 6 servings

Variation: To make Pumpkin Custard in a single dish, pour custard into 1½-quart soufflé dish instead of ramekins. Cover with foil and place in **CROCK-POT**® slow cooker. (Place soufflé dish on two or three 18×2-inch strips of foil in **CROCK-POT**® slow cooker to make removal easier, if desired.) Add water to come 1½ inches from top of soufflé dish. Cover and cook as directed.

Fruit and Nut Baked Apples

(pictured on page 106)

4 large baking apples, such as Rome Beauty or Jonathan

1 tablespoon lemon juice

⅓ cup chopped dried apricots

⅓ cup chopped walnuts or pecans

3 tablespoons packed brown sugar

½ teaspoon ground cinnamon

2 tablespoons unsalted butter, melted

½ cup water

Caramel ice cream topping (optional)

1. Scoop out center of each apple, leaving 1½-inch-wide cavity about ½ inch from bottom. Peel top of apple down about 1 inch. Brush peeled edges evenly with lemon juice. Mix apricots, walnuts, brown sugar and cinnamon in small bowl. Add butter; mix well. Spoon mixture evenly into apple cavities.

2. Pour water in bottom of **CROCK-POT®** slow cooker. Place 2 apples in bottom of **CROCK-POT®** slow cooker. Arrange remaining 2 apples above but not directly on top of bottom apples. Cover; cook on LOW 3 to 4 hours or until apples are tender. Serve warm or at room temperature with caramel ice cream topping, if desired.

Makes 4 servings

Brownie Bottoms

½ cup packed brown sugar

½ cup water

2 tablespoons unsweetened cocoa powder

2½ cups packaged brownie mix

1 package (2¾ ounces) instant chocolate pudding mix

½ cup milk chocolate chips

2 eggs, beaten

3 tablespoons butter, melted

Whipped cream or ice cream (optional)

1. Coat inside of **CROCK-POT®** slow cooker with nonstick cooking spray. Combine brown sugar, water and cocoa in small saucepan; bring to a boil over medium-high heat.

2. Meanwhile, combine brownie mix, pudding mix, chocolate chips, eggs and butter in medium bowl; stir until well blended. Spread batter in **CROCK-POT®** slow cooker; pour boiling sugar mixture over batter.

3. Cover; cook on HIGH 1½ hours. Turn off heat. Let stand 30 minutes. Top with whipped cream, if desired.

Makes 6 servings

Note: Recipe can be doubled for a 5-, 6- or 7-quart **CROCK-POT®** slow cooker.

Pineapple Rice Pudding

1 can (20 ounces) crushed pineapple in juice, undrained
1 can (13½ ounces) unsweetened coconut milk
1 can (12 ounces) evaporated milk
¾ cup uncooked Arborio rice
2 eggs, lightly beaten
¼ cup granulated sugar
¼ cup packed brown sugar
½ teaspoon ground cinnamon
¼ teaspoon salt
¼ teaspoon ground nutmeg
Toasted coconut (optional)
Fresh pineapple wedges (optional)

1. Combine crushed pineapple with juice, coconut milk, evaporated milk, rice, eggs, granulated sugar, brown sugar, cinnamon, salt and nutmeg in **CROCK-POT®** slow cooker; stir to blend. Cover; cook on HIGH 3 to 4 hours or until thickened and rice is tender.

2. Stir to blend. Serve warm or chilled. Garnish with coconut and pineapple slices.

Makes 8 servings

Note: To toast coconut, spread in a single layer in small heavy-bottomed skillet. Cook and stir over medium heat 1 to 2 minutes or until lightly browned. Remove from skillet; cool completely.

Cherry Delight

(pictured on page 106)

1 can (21 ounces) cherry pie filling
1 package (about 18 ounces) yellow cake mix
½ cup (1 stick) butter, melted
⅓ cup chopped walnuts

1. Place pie filling in **CROCK-POT®** slow cooker. Combine cake mix and butter in medium bowl. Spread evenly over pie filling. Sprinkle with walnuts.

2. Cover; cook on LOW 3 to 4 hours or on HIGH 1½ to 2 hours.

Makes 8 to 10 servings

Pineapple Rice Pudding

Fudge and Cream Pudding Cake

(pictured on page 107)

2 tablespoons unsalted butter

1 cup all-purpose flour

½ cup packed light brown sugar

5 tablespoons unsweetened cocoa powder, divided

2 teaspoons baking powder

½ teaspoon ground cinnamon

⅛ teaspoon salt

1 cup light cream

1 tablespoon vegetable oil

1 teaspoon vanilla

1½ cups hot water

½ cup packed dark brown sugar

Whipped cream or ice cream (optional)

1. Coat inside of 4½-quart **CROCK-POT®** slow cooker with butter. Combine flour, light brown sugar, 3 tablespoons cocoa, baking powder, cinnamon and salt in medium bowl. Add cream, oil and vanilla; stir well to combine. Pour batter into **CROCK-POT®** slow cooker.

2. Combine hot water, dark brown sugar and remaining 2 tablespoons cocoa in medium bowl; stir well. Pour sauce over cake batter. Do not stir. Cover; cook on HIGH 2 hours.

3. Spoon pudding cake onto plates. Serve with whipped cream, if desired.

Makes 8 to 10 servings

Apple Crumble Pot

FILLING

4 Granny Smith apples
(about 2 pounds),
cored and cut into
8 wedges *each*

⅔ cup packed dark brown
sugar

½ cup dried cranberries

2 tablespoons biscuit
baking mix

2 tablespoons butter, cubed

1½ teaspoons ground
cinnamon

1 teaspoon vanilla

¼ teaspoon ground allspice

TOPPING

1 cup biscuit baking mix

½ cup rolled oats

⅓ cup packed dark brown
sugar

3 tablespoons cold butter,
cubed

½ cup chopped pecans

Whipped cream or ice
cream (optional)

1. Coat inside of **CROCK-POT®** slow cooker with nonstick cooking spray. For filling, combine apples, ⅔ cup brown sugar, cranberries, 2 tablespoons baking mix, butter, cinnamon, vanilla and allspice in **CROCK-POT®** slow cooker; toss gently to coat.

2. For topping, combine 1 cup baking mix, oats and ⅓ cup brown sugar in large bowl. Cut in 3 tablespoons butter with pastry blender or two knives until mixture resembles coarse crumbs. Sprinkle evenly over filling in **CROCK-POT®** slow cooker. Top with pecans. Cover; cook on HIGH 2¼ hours.

3. Turn off heat. Let stand, uncovered, 15 to 30 minutes before serving. Top with whipped cream, if desired.

Makes 6 to 8 servings

Easy Peach Buckle

2 packages (16 ounces
   each) frozen peach
   slices, thawed *or*
   5 cups fresh peach
   slices
¼ cup granulated sugar
1¾ cups all-purpose flour
½ cup packed brown sugar
2 teaspoons baking powder
1 teaspoon ground
   cinnamon
1 teaspoon baking soda
¼ teaspoon salt
1⅓ cups buttermilk
6 tablespoons canola oil
1 teaspoon vanilla

1. Coat inside of 4½-quart **CROCK-POT®** slow cooker with nonstick cooking spray.

2. Toss peaches with granulated sugar; set aside.

3. Combine flour, brown sugar, baking powder, cinnamon, baking soda and salt in large bowl. Combine buttermilk, oil and vanilla in small bowl; mix well. Stir buttermilk mixture into flour mixture just until blended.

4. Spread batter evenly in **CROCK-POT®** slow cooker. Arrange peaches on batter. Cover; cook on HIGH 2½ hours or until buckle springs back when touched. Serve warm.

Makes 12 servings

tip

After cakes and breads have finished cooking, allow them to cool 5 to 10 minutes before removing them from the stoneware or baking pan.

Apple-Pecan Bread Pudding

8 cups bread, cubed

3 cups Granny Smith
    apples, cubed

1 cup chopped pecans

8 eggs

1 can (12 ounces)
    evaporated milk

1 cup packed brown sugar

½ cup apple cider or apple
    juice

2 teaspoons ground
    cinnamon

1 teaspoon ground nutmeg

1 teaspoon vanilla extract

½ teaspoon salt

½ teaspoon ground allspice

    Ice cream (optional)

    Caramel ice cream
      topping (optional)

1. Coat inside of **CROCK-POT**® slow cooker with nonstick cooking spray. Place bread cubes, apples and pecans in **CROCK-POT**® slow cooker.

2. Combine eggs, evaporated milk, brown sugar, apple cider, cinnamon, nutmeg, vanilla, salt and allspice in large bowl; mix well. Pour egg mixture in **CROCK-POT**® slow cooker. Cover; cook on LOW 3 hours. Serve with ice cream and top with caramel sauce, if desired.

Makes 8 servings

Index

A

Almonds: Green Bean Casserole, 94
Apple Crumble Pot, 119
Apple-Pecan Bread Pudding, 122
Apples
 Apple Crumble Pot, 119
 Apple-Pecan Bread Pudding, 122
 Fruit and Nut Baked Apples, 113
 Red Cabbage and Apples, 86
 Slow-Good Apples and Carrots, 104
Artichoke Pasta, 38
Artichokes: Artichoke Pasta, 38
Asian Sugar Snap Pea Soup, 14

B

Bacon
 Chili Barbecue Beans, 91
 Potato Soup, 30
 Red Cabbage and Apples, 86
 Simmered Split Pea Soup, 28
Bananas Foster, 110
Barbecue
 Chili Barbecue Beans, 91
 Pulled Chicken Sandwiches, 74
 Simple Barbecue Chicken, 74
Beans, Black
 Black and White Chili, 30
 Chili with Turkey and Beans, 20
 Mother's Sausage and Vegetable Soup, 18
Beans, Chili: Chorizo Chili, 26

Beans, Great Northern
 Black and White Chili, 30
 Chili Barbecue Beans, 91
Beans, Green: Green Bean Casserole, 94
Beans, Kidney
 Chili with Turkey and Beans, 20
 Classic Chili, 12
 Weeknight Chili, 16
Beans, Lima
 Chili Barbecue Beans, 91
 Slow-Cooked Succotash, 98
Beans, Red
 Chili Barbecue Beans, 91
 Red Beans and Rice, 72
Beef *(see also* **Beef, Ground***):* Easy Family Burritos, 78
Beef, Ground
 Beefy Tortellini, 52
 Chorizo Chili, 26
 Classic Chili, 12
 Easy Chili, 24
 Slow Cooker Pizza Casserole, 76
 Southwest-Style Meat Loaf, 60
 Super Meatball Sliders, 66
 Weeknight Chili, 16
Beefy Tortellini, 52
Black and White Chili, 30
Broccoli
 Asian Sugar Snap Pea Soup, 14
 Broccoli Rabe and Sausage Rigatoni, 54

Cream Cheese Chicken with Broccoli, 50

Garden Pasta, 42

Hearty Sausage and Tortellini Soup, 10

Broccoli Rabe and Sausage Rigatoni, 54

Brownie Bottoms, 114

Buttery Vegetable Gratin, 88

C

Cabbage: Red Cabbage and Apples, 86

Candied Sweet Potatoes, 86

Carrots

Asian Sugar Snap Pea Soup, 14

Chili with Turkey and Beans, 20

Coconut-Lime Sweet Potatoes, 102

French Carrot Medley, 90

Hearty Sausage and Tortellini Soup, 10

Potato Soup, 30

Quick and Easy Homemade Chicken and Dumplings, 64

Simmered Split Pea Soup, 28

Slow-Good Apples and Carrots, 104

Tuna Casserole, 62

Cauliflower

Cauliflower Mash, 84

Cheesy Cauliflower, 102

Cauliflower Mash, 84

Cheesy Cauliflower, 102

Cherry Delight, 116

Chicken, Breasts

Black and White Chili, 30

Cream Cheese Chicken with Broccoli, 50

Easy Parmesan Chicken, 46

Pulled Chicken Sandwiches, 74

Simple Barbecue Chicken, 74

Chicken, Thighs: Chicken Tortilla Soup, 22

Chicken, Whole: Quick and Easy Homemade Chicken and Dumplings, 64

Chicken Tortilla Soup, 22

Chili Barbecue Beans, 91

Chili with Turkey and Beans, 20

Chorizo Chili, 26

Chunky Ranch Potatoes, 104

Cinnamon Roll and Sweet 'Tater Gratin, 67

Classic Chili, 12

Coconut-Lime Sweet Potatoes, 102

Corn

Corn on the Cob with Garlic Herb Butter, 90

Escalloped Corn, 100

Slow-Cooked Succotash, 98

Sunshine Squash, 82

Vegetable-Stuffed Pork Chops, 68

Corn on the Cob with Garlic Herb Butter, 90

Cran-Orange Acorn Squash, 92

Cream Cheese Chicken with Broccoli, 50

D

Double Thick Potato-Cheese Soup, 24

E

Easy Chili, 24

Easy Family Burritos, 78

Easy Parmesan Chicken, 46

Easy Peach Buckle, 120

Escalloped Corn, 100

F

Fondue: S'mores Fondue, 110

French Carrot Medley, 90

Fruit and Nut Baked Apples, 113

Fudge and Cream Pudding Cake, 118

G

Garden Pasta, 42

Green Bean Casserole, 94

H

Ham and Cheese Pasta Bake, 54
Ham and Potato Casserole, 78
Ham and Prosciutto
Ham and Cheese Pasta Bake, 54
Ham and Potato Casserole, 78
Pasta Shells with Prosciutto, 44
Hearty Sausage and Tortellini Soup, 10

L

Leeks
Asian Sugar Snap Pea Soup, 14
Buttery Vegetable Gratin, 88

M

Mother's Sausage and Vegetable Soup, 18
Mushrooms
Beefy Tortellini, 52
Cream Cheese Chicken with Broccoli, 50
Easy Parmesan Chicken, 46
French Carrot Medley, 90
Slow Cooker Pizza Casserole, 76
Turkey Stroganoff, 53
Vegetable Pasta Sauce, 48

P

Parmesan Potato Wedges, 96
Pasta and Noodles, 32–55
Hearty Sausage and Tortellini Soup, 10
Ravioli Casserole, 70
Slow Cooker Pizza Casserole, 76
Tuna Casserole, 62
Pasta Shells with Prosciutto, 44
Peach Cobbler, 108
Peaches
Easy Peach Buckle, 120
Peach Cobbler, 108

Peas
Asian Sugar Snap Pea Soup, 14
Simmered Split Pea Soup, 28
Pecans
Apple Crumble Pot, 119
Apple-Pecan Bread Pudding, 122
Pineapple Rice Pudding, 116
Pork
Pulled Pork Sliders with Cola Barbecue Sauce, 58
Vegetable-Stuffed Pork Chops, 68
Pork, Sausage
Broccoli Rabe and Sausage Rigatoni, 54
Chorizo Chili, 26
Hearty Sausage and Tortellini Soup, 10
Ravioli Casserole, 70
Slow Cooker Pizza Casserole, 76
Potatoes *(see also* **Potatoes, Sweet***)*
Asian Sugar Snap Pea Soup, 14
Chunky Ranch Potatoes, 104
Double Thick Potato-Cheese Soup, 24
Ham and Potato Casserole, 78
Mother's Sausage and Vegetable Soup, 18
Parmesan Potato Wedges, 96
Potato Soup, 30
Quick and Easy Homemade Chicken and Dumplings, 64
Potatoes, Sweet
Candied Sweet Potatoes, 86
Cinnamon Roll and Sweet 'Tater Gratin, 67
Coconut-Lime Sweet Potatoes, 102
Potato Soup, 30
Pulled Chicken Sandwiches, 74
Pulled Pork Sliders with Cola Barbecue Sauce, 58
Pumpkin Custard, 112

Q

Quick and Easy Homemade Chicken and Dumplings, 64

R

Ravioli Casserole, 70
Red Beans and Rice, 72
Red Cabbage and Apples, 86
Rice
Asian Sugar Snap Pea Soup, 14
Cran-Orange Acorn Squash, 92
Pineapple Rice Pudding, 116
Red Beans and Rice, 72
Vegetable-Stuffed Pork Chops, 68
Roasted Tomato-Basil Soup, 28

S

Salsa
Easy Family Burritos, 78
Southwest-Style Meat Loaf, 60
Sandwiches
Pulled Chicken Sandwiches, 74
Pulled Pork Sliders with Cola Barbecue Sauce, 58
Super Meatball Sliders, 66
Simmered Split Pea Soup, 28
Simple Barbecue Chicken, 74
Slow-Cooked Succotash, 98
Slow Cooker Pizza Casserole, 76
Slow-Good Apples and Carrots, 104
S'mores Fondue, 110
Southwest-Style Meat Loaf, 60
Spaghetti and Turkey Meatballs, 36
Stuffed Manicotti, 40
Sunshine Squash, 82
Super Meatball Sliders, 66

T

Three-Pepper Pasta Sauce, 34

Tortillas
Chicken Tortilla Soup, 22
Easy Family Burritos, 78
Tuna Casserole, 62
Turkey
Chili with Turkey and Beans, 20
Mother's Sausage and Vegetable Soup, 18
Spaghetti and Turkey Meatballs, 36
Turkey Stroganoff, 53
Turkey Stroganoff, 53

V

Vegetable Pasta Sauce, 48
Vegetable-Stuffed Pork Chops, 68

W

Walnuts
Cherry Delight, 116
Coconut-Lime Sweet Potatoes, 102
Fruit and Nut Baked Apples, 113
Weeknight Chili, 16

Z

Zucchini and Squash
Buttery Vegetable Gratin, 88
Cran-Orange Acorn Squash, 92
Garden Pasta, 42
Hearty Sausage and Tortellini Soup, 10
Sunshine Squash, 82
Vegetable Pasta Sauce, 48

Metric Conversion Chart

VOLUME MEASUREMENTS (dry)

1/8 teaspoon = 0.5 mL
1/4 teaspoon = 1 mL
1/2 teaspoon = 2 mL
3/4 teaspoon = 4 mL
1 teaspoon = 5 mL
1 tablespoon = 15 mL
2 tablespoons = 30 mL
1/4 cup = 60 mL
1/3 cup = 75 mL
1/2 cup = 125 mL
2/3 cup = 150 mL
3/4 cup = 175 mL
1 cup = 250 mL
2 cups = 1 pint = 500 mL
3 cups = 750 mL
4 cups = 1 quart = 1 L

VOLUME MEASUREMENTS (fluid)

1 fluid ounce (2 tablespoons) = 30 mL
4 fluid ounces (1/2 cup) = 125 mL
8 fluid ounces (1 cup) = 250 mL
12 fluid ounces (1 1/2 cups) = 375 mL
16 fluid ounces (2 cups) = 500 mL

WEIGHTS (mass)

1/2 ounce = 15 g
1 ounce = 30 g
3 ounces = 90 g
4 ounces = 120 g
8 ounces = 225 g
10 ounces = 285 g
12 ounces = 360 g
16 ounces = 1 pound = 450 g

DIMENSIONS

1/16 inch = 2 mm
1/8 inch = 3 mm
1/4 inch = 6 mm
1/2 inch = 1.5 cm
3/4 inch = 2 cm
1 inch = 2.5 cm

OVEN TEMPERATURES

250°F = 120°C
275°F = 140°C
300°F = 150°C
325°F = 160°C
350°F = 180°C
375°F = 190°C
400°F = 200°C
425°F = 220°C
450°F = 230°C

BAKING PAN SIZES

Utensil	Size in Inches/Quarts	Metric Volume	Size in Centimeters
Baking or Cake Pan (square or rectangular)	8×8×2	2 L	20×20×5
	9×9×2	2.5 L	23×23×5
	12×8×2	3 L	30×20×5
	13×9×2	3.5 L	33×23×5
Loaf Pan	8×4×3	1.5 L	20×10×7
	9×5×3	2 L	23×13×7
Round Layer Cake Pan	8×1½	1.2 L	20×4
	9×1½	1.5 L	23×4
Pie Plate	8×1¼	750 mL	20×3
	9×1¼	1 L	23×3
Baking Dish or Casserole	1 quart	1 L	—
	1½ quart	1.5 L	—
	2 quart	2 L	—